CHECKERBOARD BIOGRAPHY LIBRARY

EXPLORERS

Sir Francis
Drake

Kristin Petrie

ABDO
Publishing Company

visit us at
www.abdopub.com

Published by ABDO Publishing Company, 4940 Viking Drive, Edina, Minnesota 55435. Copyright © 2004 by Abdo Consulting Group, Inc. International copyrights reserved in all countries. No part of this book may be reproduced in any form without written permission from the publisher.

Printed in the United States.

Cover Photos: Corbis
Interior Photos: Corbis pp. 5, 7, 9, 11, 12, 15, 17, 21, 22, 23, 25, 27, 29; North Wind pp. 13, 28

Series Coordinator: Stephanie Hedlund
Editors: Kate A. Conley, Kristin Van Cleaf
Art Direction & Cover Design: Neil Klinepier
Interior Design & Maps: Dave Bullen

Library of Congress Cataloging-in-Publication Data

Petrie, Kristin, 1970-
    Sir Francis Drake / Kristin Petrie.
      p. cm. -- (Explorers)
    Includes index.
    Summary: A biography of the English seaman and explorer who was knighted by Queen Elizabeth I for helping to make England a world power by circumnavigating the globe and raiding Spanish ships.
    ISBN 1-59197-601-4
    1. Drake, Francis, Sir, 1540?-1596--Juvenile literature. 2. Great Britain--History, Naval--Tudors, 1485-1603--Juvenile literature. 3. Great Britain--History--Elizabeth, 1558-1603--Biography--Juvenile literature. 4. America--Discovery and exploration--English--Juvenile literature. 5. Admirals--Great Britain--Biography--Juvenile literature. 6. Explorers--Great Britain--Biography--Juvenile literature. [1. Drake, Francis, Sir, 1540?-1596. 2. Explorers. 3. Admirals.] I. Title.

DA86.22.D7P47 2004
942.05'5'092--dc22
[B]   2003062927

Contents

Sir Francis Drake

In the 1500s, Spaniards discovered and took control of the West Indies and Central and South America. These discoveries made Spain the most powerful country in the world.

Spanish armies also conquered the wealthy Aztec and Inca nations. Huge **fleets** carried their treasures, as well as the land's natural resources, to Spain. Spanish government officials tried to keep the wealth for themselves.

Other European countries were displeased by this **monopoly**. Queen Elizabeth I wanted England to have some of this wealth as well. She encouraged her sea captains to attack Spanish ships and take their goods.

Francis Drake was one of these captains. He sailed around the world, obtaining vast riches along the way. His accomplishments made England wealthy and powerful.

1451
Christopher Columbus born

1485
Hernán Cortés born

1450
John Cabot born

1460
Vasco da Gama born

1491
Jacques Cartier born

Sir Francis Drake was a sea dog for Queen Elizabeth I. A sea dog was a captain who attacked Spanish ships.

Eventually, Drake was knighted. Yet, some people considered him a thief, while others thought of him as a hero. Read on to determine for yourself which of these he was.

1492
Columbus's first voyage west for Spain

1496
Cabot's first voyage for England

1493
Columbus's second voyage, attempted to colonize Hispaniola

Francis's Youth

Francis Drake was born around 1540 in Crowndale, England. Edmund Drake, Francis's father, was a tenant farmer and minister. He and his wife, whose name is unknown, had 12 sons. Francis was the oldest.

Little is known about Francis's youth. However, in the 1500s it was common for poor parents to send their children to live with rich relatives. These relatives were better able to feed and educate the children. Francis may have been sent to live with William Hawkins in Plymouth, England.

Francis did not go to school. However, he did learn to read and write. In addition, many members of the Hawkins family were sailors and traders. Francis may have begun to learn about the sea when he stayed with them.

Opposite page: Francis Drake hauled freight along the Thames River in the 1500s.

1497
Cabot's second voyage, discovered the Grand Banks; da Gama was first to sail around Africa to India

1496 or 1497
Hernando de Soto born

1498
Cabot's third voyage, may have died; Columbus's third voyage

When Francis was about 13 years old, he became an **apprentice** aboard a trading vessel. At this time, he learned all about sailing. When the vessel's captain died, he left his ship to Francis. Francis continued to haul freight. After a few years, he sold the ship.

Would You?

Would you want to leave your family to live with distant relatives? Why do you think Francis Drake was sent to live with the Hawkinses?

Slave Trading

After he sold his ship, Francis began working for a distant relative named John Hawkins. John Hawkins was a well-known slave trader. Francis hoped to find adventure while sailing for him.

In 1566, Francis made his first voyage to the New World. Hawkins had assigned Francis to one of his slave trading vessels. On the way, Francis learned how to navigate the open seas. Hawkins's ships were often attacked for their cargo, so Francis also experienced his first sea battles.

The following year, Hawkins led another trading voyage. Francis commanded the *Judith*. Sometime during the voyage, Hawkins led his ships to San Juan de Ulúa. This port is on an island off the coast of Mexico.

1502
Columbus's fourth voyage; da Gama's second voyage

1506
Columbus died

1504
Cortés sailed to the West Indies

At San Juan de Ulúa, Spaniards attacked the English **fleet**. Many of Hawkins's men were killed, and he lost all of his goods. The attack sparked a fierce hatred in the Englishmen. Francis Drake would devote the rest of his life to revenge for this attack.

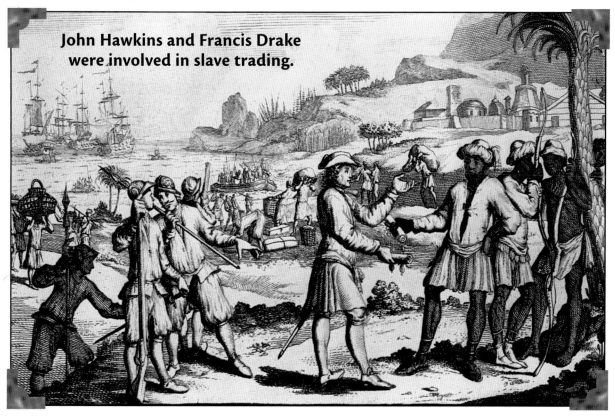

John Hawkins and Francis Drake were involved in slave trading.

1511
Cortés helped take over Cuba

1510
Francisco Vásquez de Coronado born

1514
De Soto went to the New World

Nombre de Dios

After the attack, Francis returned to England. There, he met a young woman named Mary Newman. In 1569, they married. Mary is believed to have been a commoner, as was Francis. Francis and Mary did not have children.

After the wedding, Francis continued his adventures at sea. In 1570, he sailed back to the New World. He **raided** the coastlines and Spanish ports. He found the hidden town of Nombre de Dios, Panama. There, Spanish ships were loaded with gold and silver from mines throughout the New World.

In 1572, Francis again **terrorized** the Spaniards in the New World. He overtook their richest ships and ports, including Nombre de Dios. He collected a great deal of silver and gold.

Opposite page: **Drake's fleet often attacked Spanish treasure ships.**

1524
Da Gama's third voyage, died in Cochin, India

1519–1521
Cortés conquered the Aztec Empire and claimed Mexico for Spain

1532
De Soto helped attack the Inca Empire

Would You?

Would you feel that you had gotten revenge after stealing Spanish treasures? Why do you think Drake continued stealing from the Spaniards?

Royal Expedition

Drake's accomplishments made him famous. Queen Elizabeth was impressed and chose him to lead another expedition. Drake's worldwide voyage began in December 1577.

The expedition had three main goals. One was to establish trade where Spain had not. Another was to search for a continent in the South Seas. But the most important goal was to gain more Spanish treasure.

Drake's **fleet** had five ships and fewer than 200 men. On

Queen Elizabeth I

1534
Cartier's first voyage for France

1539–1542
De Soto explored La Florida

1533
De Soto helped take over Cuzco

1535
Cartier's second voyage

December 13, the *Pelican*, *Elizabeth*, and *Marigold* set sail from Plymouth. With them were the *Swan* and the *Benedict*. Both of these ships carried supplies.

The **fleet**'s first stop was at the Cape Verde Islands near Africa. There, Drake's men overpowered two Portuguese ships. Drake made his friend, Thomas Doughty, captain of one of the captured vessels.

Ships often stopped at the Cape Verde Islands to take on supplies.

Then, the ships sailed across the Atlantic Ocean to the northeastern tip of South America. They continued down the coast. Toward the southern end of the continent, they stopped at the port of San Julián.

At San Julián, Drake heard rumors that Doughty wanted to take control of the expedition. So, Drake had his fellow captain **executed**.

At this time, Drake had the *Swan* and the *Benedict* destroyed. They were no longer needed to carry supplies. Then, the remaining ships continued south. In August 1578, Drake reached the southern point of South America.

The **fleet** passed through the Strait of Magellan. The passage took 16 days and was very difficult. Storms in this region damaged the *Marigold* beyond repair. The *Elizabeth* was blown far into the sea. Only the *Pelican* remained. Drake renamed the *Pelican* the *Golden Hind*. Then, he turned north.

This replica of the *Golden Hind* was completed in 1971. From 1977 to 1980, it honored the 400th anniversary of Drake's journey by following the same path as the original ship.

Spanish Territory

Drake was now sailing up the Pacific coast of South America. He was the first Englishman to sail in these waters. Before Drake, Spaniards had been the only European visitors on the western coast of South America.

The Spaniards did not expect to be attacked and left their harbors unprotected. So, they were easy targets for the English. Drake **raided** Spanish settlements along the coasts of what are now Chile and Peru.

In March 1579, Drake overpowered a Spanish treasure vessel called the *Cacafuego*. The English crew helped themselves to the silver, gold, and other goods. Then, they continued north.

Drake sailed as far as 48° north **latitude**. This was around today's Vancouver, Canada. He then turned south

1567
Drake's second voyage

1577
Drake began a worldwide voyage, was first Englishman to sail the Pacific Ocean

1570 and 1572
Drake terrorized the Spanish in the New World

again. He stopped at what is now San Francisco. There, Drake claimed the surrounding land for England. He called it New Albion.

In California, Drake met the Miwok Native Americans.

Would You?

Would you go into enemy territory with only one ship? How do you think Drake was able to steal so much treasure?

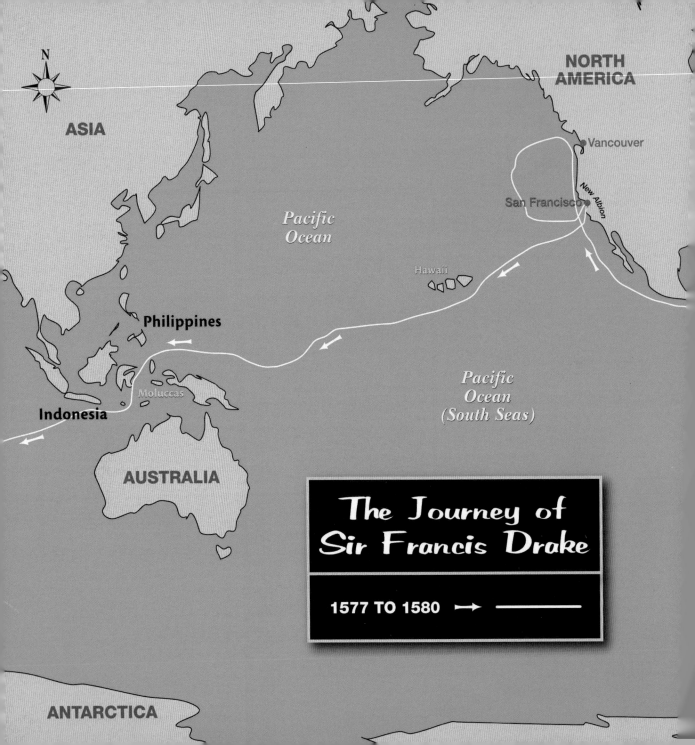

NORTH AMERICA

ASIA

Pacific Ocean

Vancouver

New Albion

San Francisco

Hawaii

Philippines

Pacific Ocean (South Seas)

Indonesia

Moluccas

AUSTRALIA

The Journey of Sir Francis Drake

1577 TO 1580 →

ANTARCTICA

England

English Channel

Crowndale
Plymouth

EUROPE

Atlantic Ocean

Cádiz

AFRICA

St. Augustine

West Indies

Hispaniola

Santo Domingo

Nombre de Dios

Panama City

Cape Verde Islands

Indian Ocean

SOUTH AMERICA

Atlantic Ocean

Cape of Good Hope

San Julián

Strait of Magellan

ANTARCTICA

Sir Knight

Drake knew Spanish ships would attack him if he sailed back around South America. So instead, he turned his ship west and crossed the Pacific Ocean.

The **fleet** stopped in the Philippines. Next, Drake made a treaty to trade valuable spices at Moluccas, also known as the Spice Islands. Then, he crossed the Indian Ocean and sailed around the tip of Africa.

Drake had sailed around the world! He reached Plymouth, England, on September 26, 1580. He presented Queen Elizabeth with spices, gold, silver, and jewels. For his work, she made Drake a knight in 1581.

For the next few years, Sir Francis Drake spent more time on land. He was now wealthy and respected. He bought an estate called Buckland Abbey. He was mayor of Plymouth from 1581 to 1584. He was also appointed to **Parliament**.

1588
Drake helped England win the Battle of Gravelines against Spain's Invincible Armada

1581
Drake knighted by Queen Elizabeth I

1596
Drake died

Mary Drake, Francis's wife of 12 years, died in 1583. Two years later, Drake married a woman named Elizabeth Sydenham. Elizabeth was from a noble, wealthy family. The couple never had any children.

Queen Elizabeth I knighted Sir Francis Drake aboard the *Golden Hind*.

1728
James Cook born

1765
Boone journeyed to Florida

1768
Cook sailed for Tahiti

1734
Daniel Boone born

1767
Boone explored Kentucky

More Raiding

In the fall of 1585, Drake was called back to sea. He took part in more **raids** in the West Indies. Queen Elizabeth ordered him to do as much damage to Spain's empire as possible. So he seized its leading settlement, Santo Domingo, Hispaniola. He also destroyed a fort at St. Augustine, Florida.

King Philip II of Spain was enraged by this fearless pirate. The king was losing his fortune! He began planning an attack against the English. He called it the Enterprise of England. In his plan, a large **fleet** called the Invincible Armada would attack the English.

Drake was told to stop the invasion. In 1587, he sailed to Cádiz, Spain. This port was where supplies for the armada were being

King Philip II

1772
Cook's second attempt to discover a seventh continent, became first man to cross the Antarctic Circle

1769
Cook's first attempt to discover a seventh continent; Boone discovered the Cumberland Gap

Cádiz, Spain

assembled. In Cádiz, Drake's 30 ships and 2,000 men sank the Spanish ships and stole weapons. Anything Spain could use in the invasion was destroyed or stolen.

In addition, they looted yet another Spanish treasure ship on the way home. However, Drake's attack only managed to delay the Spanish invasion. King Philip became more determined than ever after these embarrassing losses.

1778
Cook became the first European to record Hawaiian Islands; Boone captured by Shawnee

1775
Boone cut the Wilderness Road from Virginia to Kentucky

1779
Cook died

Invincible Armada

In the spring of 1588, the armada was finally ready. Nearly 150 warships carried 19,000 Spanish soldiers to battle. The English had about 40 warships and many smaller boats. Sir Francis Drake commanded a ship named *Revenge*.

The **fleets** met in the English Channel in July 1588. On July 27, the English sent eight ships toward the armada. They had been filled with gunpowder and then set on fire. To avoid being destroyed, the Spanish ships broke their formation and headed to sea.

Then on July 29, the Battle of Gravelines began. The English destroyed or captured many Spanish ships. Thousands of Spanish soldiers died or were taken captive. The remaining Spaniards fled to safer waters. England claimed victory.

Opposite page: **The Invincible Armada attacked England but was defeated. Fewer than half of its ships returned to Spain.**

1813
John C. Frémont born

1842
Frémont's first independent surveying mission

1820
Boone died

Fall from Favor

Sir Francis Drake was a hero again. Nevertheless, he continued to have revenge on his mind. In 1589, Drake headed for a Spanish port in Portugal. He **raided** trading ships but was unable to take over the city. Many of his crew and soldiers died on the voyage.

Queen Elizabeth was disappointed, and she lost interest in her favorite pirate. Back on land, Drake resumed his position in England's **parliament**. He **supervised** the construction of a channel that would bring freshwater to Plymouth. He also dreamed of another attack on Spain.

Six years later, Queen Elizabeth agreed to another raid. Drake and John Hawkins set sail once again for the New World in 1595. By the time the ships reached their **destination**, Drake was the lone commander. Hawkins had died while crossing the Atlantic.

1856
Frémont ran for president of the United States but lost

1845-1846
Frémont explored the Great Basin and the Pacific Coast, fought in the Mexican War

1890
Frémont died

Would you let Drake go raiding again? Why do you think Queen Elizabeth let Drake go on his final voyage?

This map shows European knowledge of North and South America during the late 1500s.

1910
Jacques Cousteau born

1951
Cousteau's first expedition in the Red Sea

1942
Cousteau and Gagnan developed the Aqua-Lung for diving

Drake's Legacy

On his last mission, Drake and his crew wiped out several Spanish ports. They also took over Nombre de Dios. Attacks on Panama City were unsuccessful, however.

By this time, Drake and many of his crew members were ill with **dysentery**. The captain continued to give orders, even from his deathbed. Sir Francis Drake died on January 28, 1596, off the coast of Panama. The crew buried their captain at sea.

Sir Francis Drake

Sir Francis Drake is remembered in good and bad ways. He was a pirate. Yet he gave this wealth to England. He was merciless with his enemies. On the other hand, he was respectful to his crew, and even to his prisoners.

To England, Sir Francis Drake was a hero. He was ambitious and courageous. He sailed into unknown waters, increasing the knowledge of the world. Drake helped his country become a world power.

This statue of Sir Francis Drake stands in Plymouth, England.

Glossary

apprentice - a person who learns a trade or craft from a skilled worker.

destination - the place someone or something is going to.

dysentery - a disease of the intestines.

execute - to put to death according to law.

fleet - a group of ships under one command.

latitude - a measure of distance north and south on the earth's surface. This distance is shown on a map by lines that run parallel to the equator.

monopoly - the complete control of a product, service, or industry.

parliament - the highest lawmaking body of some governments.

raid - a sudden attack.

supervise - to watch over and take care of something.

terrorize - to fill with terror and anxiety.

Saying It

Cádiz - KAH-theeth
dysentery - DIH-suhn-tehr-ee
Moluccas - moh-LUH-kuhz
Nombre de Dios - NAWM-bray thay THEE-ohs
San Juan de Ulúa - sahn WAHN thay oo-LOO-ah

Web Sites

To learn more about Sir Francis Drake, visit ABDO Publishing Company on the World Wide Web at **www.abdopub.com**. Web sites about Sir Francis Drake are featured on our Book Links page. These links are routinely monitored and updated to provide the most current information available.

Index